# IF YOU JAM THE COPIER, BOLT!

ALSO BY STEVE ALTES

*The Little Book of Bad Business Advice*

# IF YOU JAM THE COPIER, BOLT!

## And Other Ways to Drive Your Coworkers Crazy

**Steve Altes**

**Andrews McMeel Publishing**

Kansas City

01 02 03 04 05 BIN 10 9 8 7 6 5 4 3 2 1

ISBN: 0-7407-1865-7

Library of Congress Catalog Card Number: 2001089272

*For Tiffni, my Muse of Fire*

# ACKNOWLEDGMENTS

Aiding persons in the birthing of books is an act punishable by acknowledgment.

So thank you, Jeff Herman, literary superagent, for plucking my manuscript from behind the tattered couch of oblivion.

Hats off to Pete Gasparini, Chris Jalbert, Matt Terrigno, and Sam Murray, from whose minds sprang the funniest maxims in this book.

Special thanks to all the despicable bosses I've had for catalyzing this manifesto. Any similarity between the advice in this book and the actions of actual persons is purely intentional.

My deepest thanks go to the world's sexiest woman, the callipygous Tiffni Diana Jellinek: You are my inspiration, my coconspirator, my love goddess.

Lastly, I'd like to thank myself for writing this book. I couldn't have done it without me.

# INTRODUCTION

Sequels reek, don't they? Just as sure as embarrassment follows the company Christmas party, a best-selling management advice book will spawn a dreary, repetitive sequel—mostly just a repackaging of the first book. *In Search of Excellence* led to *A Passion for Excellence*. *Leadership Secrets of Attila the Hun* begat *Victory Secrets of Attila the Hun*. A franchise is created and the unsuspecting book-buying public gobbles up anything the "guru" spews out—fresh insights or not. Great for the author's bank account, but not very helpful to the reader.

I would have none of this, so I threw out the existing bad business paradigms and started with a clean sheet of paper. I took new jobs and discovered fresh ways to drive my bosses and coworkers crazy. You deserve no less. Four years and eleven jobs later, this is what I learned. . . .

*Ask your boss if she has put on a few pounds recently.*

**In a difficult situation, when you ask yourself, "What's the worst that can happen?" the answer probably is, "A catastrophe of biblical proportions."**

*Show up for a complex number-crunching session with a credit card–sized calculator.*

**The more office furniture you have, the higher your status. Snag an extra chair from the conference room and watch your power grow. Covet thy neighbor's credenza!**

*By the age of thirty-three, Thomas Jefferson penned the Declaration of Independence. At twenty-six, Albert Einstein conceived the theory of relativity. Joan of Arc led the French army at seventeen. How old are you? What have you done lately?*

Create an angry workplace where unappreciated employees toil on soulless tasks for hostile bosses in hermetically sealed buildings for slave wages.

*Leave your resume in the copier.*

*Delegate the dull,
dirty work and keep the
stimulating jobs for yourself.*

**Pick a day planner full
of extraneous crap like
parcel post rates, foreign
holidays, and the amount
of rainfall in Bolivia.**

Constantly spam your colleagues. "Hey, everybody! I swear this is true: A friend of mine was charged $250 for a chocolate chip cookie recipe by this department store. That is just so unfair. Here's the recipe. . . . "

*Lead a life of
quiet desperation.*

**Protest company Christmas
displays. Insist that only
"nondenominational"
holiday decorations be used.**

*Quote Karl Marx and Friedrich Engels a lot.*

**Dredge up fifty-year-old scientific papers on arcane topics and highlight random sections. Send them to your boss with a note saying, "Thought you better take a look at this."**

**Make important business decisions with a Tyco Magic 8 Ball.**

*Treat employees like pond scum, but hang posters that say "We Value Our Employees."*

**Wallow in a sea of past regrets. Make "If only I had . . ." lists.**

*Tell your boss that as a feng shui practitioner, you must have a corner office. If he hassles you, remind him that he can't discriminate against you based on your religion.*

Bring a huge duffel bag as carry-on luggage and board the plane the instant the flight attendant calls for passengers with "special needs." If she asks, say your special need is to "beat the other slobs in the race to hog the overhead bin."

*Hire people with book smarts,
not common sense.*

You are the Master of your
Fate, the Captain of your
Soul! Carpe diem! Oops,
sorry. Actually you're not.
Turns out you're really a
drone. Return to your
cubicle and be quiet.

Corporations must change to survive. Create a Corporate Change Department to handle this.

*End every sentence with ". . . quoth the Raven" or ". . . according to prophecy."*

Squander vast corporate resources trying to win government quality awards.

*If your boss's desk is neat and orderly, make Freudian comments about his "anal fixation."*

*"A" student in college? Relax! You're guaranteed to succeed in the real world.*

**Let eye gunk and dust build up to a nice haze on your glasses.**

*Fix the blame,
not the problem.*

**Speech tip: Write out
your speech beforehand
and read it word for
word in a monotone voice
without looking at the
audience while jingling
coins in your pockets.**

**The thicker your briefcase,
the higher your status.**

*Move your chair next to
the printer and sit there all
day reading the newspaper.
If anyone asks, just say
you are waiting for a
huge print job.*

**Let out an exasperated sigh whenever your boss enters your office.**

*If an underling says he needs time off for a relative's funeral, don't believe him. Make him produce the obituary.*

*Before faxing, pick up the
handset and shriek fax sounds
into it to "kick-start" it.*

**The best way to relieve
office stress is to eat a
big plate of greasy food,
drink lots of alcohol,
and go to sleep.**

*Incubate colorful new life forms in your coffee cup.*

**Transform the office refrigerator into a scary cave of rotting fruit and forgotten sandwiches, congealed pizza from the last office party, and fermenting paper bags no one dares open.**

When you can't find something, your first reaction should be to immediately accuse your boss of borrowing it without permission.

*If your boss asks you to work late, tell him you can't because the "office is scary at night."*

Physical setup is very important in negotiations. Arrange it so you sit in a high-backed, black leather chair, while your adversary sits in a tiny Playskool chair with sticky armrests facing the sun. Offer him apple juice in a sippie-cup and shout: *"I* AM THE ALPHA DOG! *I* AM THE ALPHA DOG!"

**Bring nothing to
read on the plane.
Sit there and stew.**

*Clench your jaw, twitch
your eyes, and snort every
time someone mentions a
competitor's name.*

*Name an important project "Project Basura" and store all its papers in a box labeled "Basura." The next day scream bloody murder after Spanish-speaking janitors mistake it for trash and haul it away.*

Bury your head in a report and walk through the halls at top speed, making people jump out of your way. And walk on the *left* for a change. You're not a car, after all.

*Why be part of the solution when you can be part of the problem?*

*Run during lunch and drape your nasty shorts over the doorknob to air out.*

**"To-do" lists are a crutch. Mentally keep track of what you have to do. That's what your brain is for.**

**First thing every morning, call a meeting to discuss the day's commute.**

*Spend flagrantly at year-end to ensure you have no money left over in your budget. If you show a surplus, they'll just cut your budget for next year.*

*Pass the time on long plane flights by spying on the laptop of the person next to you. If this is done to you, type, "Dear Diary: I am trying so hard not to strangle the idiot next to me. Oh, Lord, stop me before I kill again."*

*Refer to notes on your hand during job interviews.*

Criticize the ideas and creations of others. People love hearing that their children are ugly.

When someone copies a page from a magazine, book, or newsletter, ask if they received permission from the publisher. If they didn't, place them under citizen's arrest for copyright infringement and try to collect a reward.

*Make your office look like a Tijuana souvenir shop filled with dopey stuffed animals, tacky business card holders, dreary coffee mugs, and pens that strip when you tilt them.*

**Schedule "Employee Appreciation Day" for November 31.**

*Winnie-the-Pooh, Attila the Hun, and Rogue Warriors have lots to teach us about management.*

**Order messy finger foods like fried chicken and barbecued ribs at business lunches.**

Want to be promoted to
senior vice president?
Follow this surefire process.
First: Figure out what you
need to do in order to be
promoted. Second: Do it.

*Discipline employees by making
them sniff the inside of the
office microwave oven.*

**Demonstrate your excellent editing skills by sending your boss heavily marked up versions of memos he has already sent out.**

*See that your monkeys jump on your boss's back.*

*Tell computer novices that a great way to back up their important computer files is to type "format c:\".*

**Issue a preemptive memo detailing your "No Sex During Staff Meetings" policy.**

Reject rejection letters. Write them back: "I regret to inform you that I am unable to accept your refusal to offer me employment. This year I have received an unusually large number of rejection letters, making it impossible for me to accept them all. Despite your outstanding experience in rejecting applicants, your refusal does not meet with my needs at this time. Therefore, I shall initiate employment with your firm immediately. Best of luck in rejecting future candidates."

**Tout your product's features, not its benefits.**

*Stamp invoices: "Invoices one day late will be turned over to the Gambino crime family for collection."*

Give bizarre directions to your office. "Take the road out of town. After sixty-three oak trees, turn at the store. Drive four kilometers to the building with windows on the sides and a roof on top. That's us."

*Spice up maps to your office with spots marked "my secret hiding place," "Bigfoot's lair," "buried treasure," and "portal to Romulan Empire."*

**Tell your boss there's a camera crew from *60 Minutes* waiting outside his office.**

Hand out business cards
printed on a laser printer.
There's just no better
way to say "I won't be
in business very long."

When a staffer goes on
vacation or a honeymoon, ask
for phone numbers where he
can be reached at all times.

*Tape a picture of Saddam Hussein to your ID badge and see how many weeks it takes that eagle-eyed security guard to notice.*

**Carry a stack of *People* magazines into the rest room and tell your secretary to hold your calls for an hour.**

Have a "don't ask,
don't tell" policy with your
boss. If he doesn't *ask* you
to do anything, you won't
*tell* him to shove it.

*Wait until you lose your job
before looking for another.*

Spark your creativity by making little changes in your daily routine, like speaking only in pig latin, eating lunch without using your hands, or wearing your pants backward.

*Leave the copier set for enlarge 165%, extra dark, stapled, 11" x 17" paper, 99 copies.*

*Working late? Indulge in
lascivious fantasies about
the cleaning staff.*

**Swarm new hires and
chant like a zombie:
"Surrender your personality.
You will be assimilated.
Resistance is futile."**

*Remember: Your past
equals your future.*

Your wife's artistic, right?
Let her design the new
company logo! The perfect
way to blend your work
life and your home life
for the benefit of all.

Charge any time you spend thinking about work to your time sheet, even if you're at home or at the beach.

*To liven up a boring meeting, jump on the conference table, shadowbox, and meow until they physically restrain you.*

Underbid contracts and tell yourself, "Sure, we'll lose a little bit on each one, but we'll make it up in volume."

*Leave wacky greetings on your answering machine, complete with dog barks, banjo music, and your three-year-old daughter's voice.*

*So the company gypped you at bonus time. Stop complaining and steal a few thousand dollars' worth of pencils. There, you're even. Get back to work.*

**If you have time to do things right the first time, you have too much time on your hands.**

*If a supply clerk gets in your way, hit him with "Why do you worry about employee theft? This is an office, not a diamond mine! What do you think you're protecting? The Hope Paper Clip? The Star of India Ink?"*

Constantly send e-mails
to the entire company
keeping them up to the
minute on your activities.
"I'll be in the bathroom
if anyone needs me."

*Recycle used mailing tubes.*
*Use them as trumpets,*
*telescopes, and swords.*

When you leave work, leave your light and computer on. Then put a second briefcase, identical to your regular one, on your desk to make it look like you're still around, working late. For extra realism, lay a spare set of keys on top.

*Immediately go for the maximum recline in airplane seats while using your knee to block the guy in front of you from doing the same.*

**Call 1-900-HOT-ORGY from your corporate rival's phone when he's not around.**

# Fawn, brownnose, and boot lick.

*Tell your staff that failure is the ultimate sin and you will not tolerate even the smallest mistake so they better not take any risks.*

*Ask the guy in the neighboring cubicle if he could possibly think more quietly.*

**Gamble the rent money on a get-rich-quick scheme you saw on a 3:00 A.M. infomercial.**

Send colleagues a somber
e-mail saying you have a
brain tumor. After every-
one sends you flowers and
presents, send another
e-mail saying it wasn't
a tumor after all, just a
really bad hangover.

Conduct scientific experiments at work, like how much is "too much" coffee, how long can a glue stick survive the microwave, and how many sheets of paper does it take to permanently jam the three-hole punch.

*Cram plants into your office until it looks like the Amazon, then neglect them. This brown, sickly sight is the perfect way to send the message "I just don't care anymore."*

**Let sunk costs influence future spending decisions. Throw good money after bad.**

Want to snooze at work? Spread hundreds of paper clips on your office floor, lie down with your feet next to the door, and go to sleep. If anyone comes in, just pretend you were picking up paper clips.

**Refer to people as belly buttons. "I just don't have enough *belly buttons* to throw at this project."**

*Keep three months' salary in the bank in case you're fired. No, wait. Why just three months'? Keep three years' salary in the bank.*

*Try to bribe auditors and inspectors with a crisp, new one-dollar bill.*

Change your company's name to "Some Random Fly-by-Night Company." Think of the fun other companies will have announcing they are awarding contracts to you.

*Hawaiian shirts, halter tops, and flip-flops. All excellent choices for Casual Day.*

**Prominently display pinup calendars like "Beach Vixens" and "Sizzling Firemen" in your office.**

When shopping for home-office equipment, consider getting the same printer and fax that your office uses. It'll make swiping compatible supplies that much easier.

*"Pile on" other people's charge numbers.*

**Nay-say, pooh-pooh,
and bear ill will.**

*When asked for a rough order
of magnitude price quote, give
an incredibly low number.
Then, for the firm quote,
double it. Technically, it's still
within an order of magnitude.*

*Ask colleagues: "If you're so smart . . .*

- *why don't you have my job?"*

- *why aren't you rich?"*

- *why are you working here?"*

**Grab your boss's attention by FedEx-ing him your memos. Even if he's just down the hall.**

When your boss tells you about an upcoming task, say to him in "robot" voice: "Yes, master, I eagerly await this important assignment. I look forward to diligently working on all your urgent issues."

When coworkers scarf down doughnuts, tell them that each one has five hundred calories and count their calories aloud, bite by bite.

*Locate the visitors' parking lot as far from the building entrance as possible.*

Make a workplace bingo card, with squares like "Office grouch moans he's swamped," "Coffeepot left empty," "Network crashes," "Coworker displays zero fashion sense." Mark one every time it happens and see how long it takes to fill a line.

*Use euphemisms for "firing."
Call it "resume revision days,"
"retroactive hiring freeze," or
"excreting corporate waste."*

**Post your computer
password on your monitor.**

**When delegating, specify not only what you want, but _exactly_ how it is to be done.**

_Before trimming your nose hairs or pulling long strings of gum from your mouth during meetings, turn your chair around so the others can't see you._

*Walk the halls muttering
to yourself, "They're all out
to get me," and "Be quiet!
They'll hear you."*

**Try to convert your boss
to your religion.**

Post gloomy messages on the company bulletin board. Famine, war, illness, and death are excellent topics. If people complain, say, "Okay, Pollyanna, go on living in your fantasy world, where none of this stuff exists. Go back to that oh-so-important report. Don't let me disturb you."

Any time you fail to deliver as promised, blame it on the network. "The server was down and I couldn't access my files or the printer."

*Hang a "Do Not Disturb" sign on your office door. Hope that people will respect your wishes and leave you alone for a few years.*

Most professional women will never admit it, but deep down they *love* being called "Doll Face," "Cupcake," "Biscuit," and "Hottie" in business settings.

*When your boss calls, put him on hold and walk away.*

*During back-to-school season, take your children to your office supply room for a little "midnight requisition."*

**Cut in front of people in the office cafeteria, saying, "Business is cutthroat. Law of the jungle! It's you or me, baby!"**

*Live your life as though
it's just a rehearsal for your
real life yet to come.*

**Ferret out industrial spies
in your organization.
Interrogate everyone.
It's a safe bet that
anyone who challenges
you is really a spy.**

**Chide your boss,
"When I have your job,
I'm going to do things
a lot differently."**

*When your boss walks by your
office, furtively open a desk
drawer, peer in, and say, "Got
enough air in there, little guy?"*

Needle coworkers with
hyphenated names.
Does she really think "Ms.
Griswold-Brunschwyler"
has a nice ring to it?
Call her "Ms. Griswold-
Stop-Wasting-My-Life-
Pronouncing-Your-Stupid-
Last-Name-Brunschwyler"
from now on.

**Every day, strive to
make the workplace
a little less human.**

*Never give your boss progress
reports. Wait until he asks,
"What the hell have you been
doing for the last six months?"
before you tell him anything.*

When assigning boring tasks to your staff, inspire them with "A hundred years from now, it won't matter what your bank account was, what kind of house you lived in, or what kind of car you drove. But the world may be a little bit nicer because you took the time to . . . type this memo, clean the fry-o-later, scrape chewing gum off the parking lot, whatever."

Refer to yourself in the third person. "Donna, it would make Bob very happy if you made Bob five copies of this report."

*Spend the first four hours at the office planning your day's work.*

*Explain to your subordinates that the reason their bonuses were so small this year was so that your bonus could be "so colossal."*

**Forget to return the visitor's badge.**

Stroke your fragile ego by taking pride in the accomplishments of your company. Tell yourself that you had something to do with it, even though everybody knows you didn't.

*Chew borrowed pens.*

*Tell your staff not to refer to you as their "boss" or "supervisor." Suggest that they call you "Conquistador," "Overlord," or "Flavius Bizmacticus" instead.*

**Leave a copy of *Mein Kampf* on your desk.**

When people leave work before you, call out, "Weakling! Couldn't handle it, huh? Couldn't stay for the long haul. Go home to your bottle, little baby. I'll just stay here, *working late.*"

*Trust statistics.*

The night of March 31, send your company's major investors a fake press release saying the company is "declaring bankruptcy due to massive embezzlement." Everybody loves a good April Fool's Day prank.

Answer all presentation questions with, "Gee, that's an interesting question. I'll have to get back to you on that." Of course, you never do.

*Take a penny; never leave a penny. Hell, take a handful. Even if you didn't buy anything.*

**Problems are best solved when they're monstrously complicated, no-win situations; not when they're little.**

*Display hideous drawings in your office. If people make disparaging comments about them, say, "Thanks a lot. My kid drew that for me."*

*Tip waiters in leftover foreign currency.*

**Every day complain to the office manager that the soda machine ripped you off. You can pocket an extra hundred bucks a year this way.**

*Give moist handshakes.*

**Make a big stink over the service during business lunches. Send the food back several times. Your colleagues will respect your uncompromising nature.**

Turn your office into an
"I Love Me" shrine.
Decorate it with clippings
and photos of yourself.
Install a trophy case.

*Organize a carpool.*
*On your day, show up at*
*your colleague's house*
*on a motorcycle.*

On the memo line of your checks, write things like "narcotics shipment," "Klan dues," and "hush money."

*When you leave a message, never say what your call is regarding.*

*Pretend you don't remember how to use your stapler. Insist that you're not kidding and have someone demonstrate it for you.*

**Bring a pillow and sleeping cap to staff meetings.**

*Hold premeeting meetings to plan upcoming meetings and postmeeting meetings to relive the highlights of past meetings.*

**If your boss experiences a setback or crisis, explain to him, "That's because bad things happen to bad people."**

Prohibit employees from displaying bumper stickers on their cars because they might offend someone.

*View every challenge as a potential doomsday.*

People say they appreciate punctuality, but actually they think it's cool when people show up late. They secretly wish they had the guts to do that.

*Whenever you are in a tense business setting, ask yourself, "How can I add more stress to this situation?"*

Put a sign on your door saying, "The next person to walk through this door gets a spanking."

Spend lots of time fooling around with the latest technological gadgets. If it beeps, chirps, has LCDs, or an antenna, you need it.

*Hide your agenda.*

**When asked what your salary requirements are, if you say, "Supersize it, please," they have to give you an extra $5,000 a year.**

Write your memos using only one sentence, even if that sentence is two pages long.

When coworkers ask how you are, don't say "fine" or "all right." Be truthful. Try "wretched," "bored," or "homicidal."

**Give them a full day's work the day they pay you what you deserve.**

*Fear computers. Did you know that if you push one wrong key, they can explode?*

*Bring your wife with you to job interviews to analyze how your answers come across.*

**Cap executive salaries at $400,000 because that is how much the president of the United States makes.**

*Put elaborate locks on the copier requiring special access codes. When someone asks to make a copy, raise your eyebrows as if they just asked for the launch codes to our nuclear arsenal.*

Before a meeting ask that everyone turn off their beepers, cell phones, and watch alarms because those sounds can trigger your epilepsy. If someone forgets, fake a seizure.

*Refuse to read any memos unless they are written in iambic pentameter.*

Act surprised when you learn anything personal about a coworker. "Gosh, Laura, you play tennis? I only know you as the time sheet signer. I thought your whole world revolved around signing time sheets. Hell, I figured you stayed up late at night reading *Time Sheet Signers* magazine."

*When an obese person says they can handle a business situation, ask, "Why should I trust your ability to control this situation when you can't even control what you shove down your own pie hole?"*

**Outsource your core competencies.**

*If you discover someone using unlicensed software, handcuff them to their desk, call the Software Publishers Association's antipiracy hot line at (800) 388-7478, and turn them in.*

Urge coworkers to actually use those protective toilet seat covers because you have a "really nasty boil."

Whenever you receive a business gift, ask how much it cost so you can report it as miscellaneous income to the IRS.

*When stealing office supplies, remember that large items, like color laser copiers, can be taken one piece at a time.*

You are an impostor.
You got where you are by
accident. Live in daily fear
that the company will
realize you are a fraud,
end this ridiculous charade,
and fire you on the spot.

*Stiff the donation cup for
coffee and doughnuts.*

Count the number of times people say "touch base" in a meeting. For every four, scream, "Home run," and run around the room.

**With great fanfare, announce glorious new initiatives to make work easier. Then let them die of neglect a few weeks later.**

You never know if someone you fire will try to wreak havoc on the computers, so it's best to get them out of the building before dropping the ax. "Umm, Derek, can you come outside with me for a minute, please?" Then slam the door and lock them out.

When you walk by other people's offices, peer in with a look that says, "Hiding something?"

*Nothing wraps up a job interview better than a long, rambling conspiracy theory followed by "You're one of them, aren't you?"*

*Gather some people in your office and start talking loudly about your boss. When he hears his name and sticks his head in, glare at him and leave the room in silence.*

**Two words:** *chair-iot races.*

Spend the first month on a new job decorating your office. Hire wallpaperers, choose carpeting, order custom furniture, and hang track lighting. Then demand another office.

*Make your own reserved parking space with orange traffic cones.*

Jazz up your ad copy with these eye-catching phrases:

- now with fewer bloodworms
- savings from child labor passed on to you
- full of carcinogenic goodness
- endorsed by the Antichrist
- fosters Darwinian evolution via mutations

- cadaver-flavored
- preferred by four out of five pedophiles
- chock-full-o'-asbestos
- puppy-tested
- Hitlerian efficiency

*Lead by dictum,
not example. You didn't
work hard all those years just
so you can slave away like
the wretches beneath you.*

**Evaluate your staff with
impersonal software
programs that use multiple
choice responses to generate
form letter evaluations.**

Mark every fax and e-mail "urgent." People like to spice up their boring days by pretending they're handling urgent messages.

At bonus time, quiz your staff with photos of the janitors. Those who can identify the janitors by name must be working long hours and should get the biggest bonuses.

**Tell obvious lies to
your boss about trivial
things like the weather
and the time of day.**

*If morale is low, issue a memo
directing employees to increase
morale or face termination.*

Find an unattended PC and hit Alt-Shift-PrintScreen simultaneously, putting a bitmap image of the screen in the Clipboard. Then open the Clipboard Viewer. When the person returns, he'll think he's still in his program, but everything will be frozen. Offer to solve his problem for $10.

When you botch a recipe at home, don't toss it. Bring it to work the next day as a "special treat" for your colleagues.

*When a coworker does something that bothers you, assume that they are seeking to destroy you.*

Do you:

- wear apparel from the company store?

- eat in the company cafeteria?

- go on company-sponsored recreational outings?

- date someone from inside the company?

If you answered "yes" to two or more of these questions, you have no life.

*In job interviews project
an air of nervous insecurity
balanced by a sense of
suspicious unreliability.*

**Believe that management
cares about you as a person,
not just as a worker.**

**Proposals:** Your chance to describe a fairy-tale land where magic elves work hours of uncompensated overtime to create excellence for your client in record time.

*Leave the bathroom with drips on your crotch.*

*Leave 'em guessing at the next meeting with, "I want to touch base with you to make sure we're on the same page and not wrapped around the axle. The ball's in our court, so before we get our ducks in a row, let's run this up the flagpole and see who salutes. The train's left the station and we're not on it, so let's take this off-line."*

*Don't miss out on all those wonderful behind-the-building breaks. If you don't already, take up smoking.*

**Ask female applicants: "If I hire you, how do I know you're not going to run off, get pregnant, have a baby, and want to stay home? I'd have to find someone new to fill your spot."**

*Judge documents solely on the basis of how pretty they are formatted.*

Save money when producing company catalogs: Instead of professional models, use your employees. Those ugly bastards will do just fine.

When a colleague is out for the day, turn on his computer, open up Solitaire, and put a note on his desk saying, "Catching a matinee at the multiplex. Back soon. Don't touch my game."

*Remember: Successful people are just luckier than you.*

Every day say one of the following:

- "That'll never work."

- "It's against our policy."

- "That's impossible."

- "We've always done it this way."

*Fire the payroll staff and, on payday, put one big pile of cash on a table for each employee to take out their correct salary.*
*Hey, it could work.*

**In a job interview, change your accent with every response.**

*Pay employees in company scrip. "Here's your week's pay, Dick: twenty company logo baseball caps, five tote bags, and a bag of day-old Otis Spunkmeyer cookies."*

**Mistake motion for progress.**

Clutter your desk with personal detritus until it looks like a museum exhibit: "My Dull Life: A Retrospective of the Past Decade."

Show up late for an important meeting, burst into the room, grab the phone, dial a number, and blurt out, "It's me! It's me! Don't pay the ransom! I've escaped!"

When a staffer has a personal problem (nasty divorce, death in the family), pile on the projects. He'll appreciate the chance to throw himself into his work.

*Demand that your e-mail address be sex.maniac@yourcompany.com.*

*Nickel-and-dime customers to death. "The base price is $99, but with tax, insurance, shipping, handling, and manhandling that'll be $299. And you'll need our special power cord to plug it in. That's another $50."*

*Ask your secretary to back up your entire twenty gigabyte hard drive onto floppy disks every night for you.*

**Throw food refuse in the white paper recycling container. It helps the paper biodegrade.**

# Write and mail letters when you are angry.

*Open negotiations with bluffs and empty threats followed by a series of unilateral concessions and "final" offers. Conclude by telling your opponent to "pound sand."*

*Add suffixes to colleagues'*
*"In" and "Out" signs.*

*I am In-sane, In-ebriated,*
*In-satiable, In-ert, In-solvent.*

*I am Out of my mind,*
*Out-lawed, Out-smarted,*
*Out of the closet.*

**Fire employees the day**
**before they qualify**
**for retirement.**

Describe your product to federal procurement officials as "not great, but good enough for government work."

*Page yourself over the intercom. Don't disguise your voice.*

Perk up your ears for coworkers making personal calls. Listen for their voices to get soft and low, then be silent and hang on every word.

*Show your boss you're not a "yes-man." Shoot down his proposals and disagree with everything he says.*

*Get people to finish projects by going into their offices and saying, "Is it done yet? Is it done yet? Is it done yet? Is it done yet? Is it done yet?" until they finish it.*

Conduct "blame-storming" sessions where you sit in a group discussing who to blame for your project's failure.

*Shower your boss with "confetti" from your three-hole punch every morning. Tell him it's your way of "honoring him."*

**Serve clients coffee in tacky stained mugs that proclaim "World's Greatest Lover" or "Bitch on Wheels."**

Commuting tips:

- Loathe the guy in front of you.

- Honk and swear like a maniac.

- Fume at every red light.

- Have two speeds: foot floored on the gas and foot floored on the brake.

- Listen to a cassette tape of your boss barking orders at you.

*Call the computer department and say, "Can you show me where to put the paper in the typewriter on my desk? You know, the flat typewriter with the TV attached?"*

**Psychoanalyze your boss as he tries to give you assignments.**

Charge time you spend exercising at lunch to the company because it helps you work that much more efficiently.

*Press random numbers on your touch-tone phone when speaking with customers. Ask them to stop doing that.*

When someone's computer malfunctions, suggest that replacing the mouse pad will solve the problem.

*Say "Great Caesar's Ghost" a lot and ask people to call you "Chief."*

If your boss gives you lots of work, tell yourself it's because he hates you. If he doesn't give you much work, tell yourself he's trying to show you're not needed, so he can fire you. Because he hates you.

When your boss assigns you a task, some good responses are:

- "I'll get on it as soon as I'm done with my own personal business."

- "Sorry, I don't do dog work."

- "I'll have that for you . . . the day after never."

- "Need me to bail you out again, huh?"

- "Do you want fries with that?"

- "Fine, but you'll have to sign a waiver."

- "That's another thing I'm not gonna do."

- "Can't. That would use lots of paper and I can't bear to kill that many trees."

- "You again? But you were just in here yesterday giving me work."

- "I'd love to, but I'm really swamped today. I have to sharpen my pencil, get lunch, and *mail a letter.*"

Order a bunch of stuff from a vendor. When he asks how you'll be paying for it, say you'll pay for it as soon as the patent office recognizes your "antigravity belt."

*Brew high-octane coffee in the decaf pot.*

Your office uses coffee, paper towels, Sweet 'n Low, toilet paper, sugar, creamer, paper plates, and plastic utensils, doesn't it? Well, cross them off your shopping list. Work: It's not just for stealing *office* supplies anymore.

*Follow your boss around, wearing a gas mask and spraying disinfectant on everything he touches.*

**Propose that your company create a new division—the Paper Clip Ordering Division—and put you in charge.**

**Entertain colleagues at the company diversity sensitivity seminar with your Buckwheat impersonation.**

*If your boss asks you questions about your work, start to cry and ask him why he is punishing you.*

**Label your product
"Dolphin-Safe, Cruelty-
Free, and Recyclable,
but Totally Destroys the
Rain Forest."**

*File everything in one gigantic
folder labeled "Miscellaneous."*

*Networking: Ask someone for their business card, then avoid all contact with them until you need a huge favor. "Hi, Alan, it's me, Steve. We met at that trade show in '93. Well, enough chitchat. Hire me?"*

Photocopy your butt. Photocopy a picture of your boss. Scan both into PhotoShop. Morph one into the other, stop halfway, and print the result. Voilà: the incredible ass-boss-monster-man!

*Following the rules is
more important than
getting the job done.*

**Hold the last person to quit
or be fired responsible for
everything that goes wrong.**

*A difficult problem can often be solved by reducing it to the simple question: "How would an all-knowing, all-powerful genie with a variety of superpowers and access to a time machine handle this?"*

*Use the load drawer of your computer's CD-ROM drive as a cup holder.*

**Use abstract talk rather than real-life examples and anecdotes to illustrate your points.**

Auction off your office furniture, pocket the dough, and tell your boss, "I am performing a complex financial transaction beyond your ken known as a corporate asset liquidation."

*A manager should oversee no more than two people.*

*Have new hires spend their first few weeks on the job standing around watching everybody else work.*

**Use the word "freaking" in every sentence.**

*Master the art of using Alt-Tab to switch from a computer game to a work file when the boss approaches.*

**Form a task force to study how the federal government operates. Model your company after that.**

Assign all the meeting action items to people who aren't there to defend themselves.

*Pour a glass of bleach into your computer once a month to protect it from viruses.*

Speak in a Zen koan style at work. People will think you are very wise.

Boss: "What time is the strategy meeting?"

You: "Where does time go when it passes?"

Boss: "Have you seen my printout?"

You: "How can it come to you if you are so busy seeking it?"

When you quit a job,
invent imaginary "principles"
and tell your boss that's why
you are leaving. "I demand
a ten-hour workweek,
a secretary for my secretary,
and a unicorn skin rug!
What? You refuse? I've had
it with this place! I quit!"

*Complicate, complicate, complicate.*

When your office has a "Toys for Tots" campaign, donate sweaters, instead of toys. Kids love sweaters.

If you are beautiful, you can coast through life. Only unattractive people have to work hard.

When you quit, go in style. Strut into your boss's office with Steam's "Na Na Hey Hey Kiss Him Good-bye" blasting from a boom box.

## Assume.

*Do your busy work first
thing in the morning when
you are fresh. Save your more
difficult and creative tasks
for the end of the day when
you are exhausted.*

*Ask a barber whether you need a haircut, a mechanic whether you need a tune-up, and a consultant whether you need his services.*

**Spend 1 percent of the time writing the memo and 99 percent tinkering with the fonts and layout.**

Call the chief financial officer at home at 3:00 A.M. Tell him you just had a dream where a wise owl told you the company "could increase profits—*who, who*—if only you increased revenues and lowered expenses—*who, who*." Ask if he thinks there is anything to it.

*Handle each piece of paper only once. If it is urgent, act on it immediately. If it is important but not urgent, file it for later. If it annoys you, set it on fire, toss it into the hallway, and swear at it.*

**After every business meal say: "Why don't you pick up this one and I'll get the next one?"**

*Warn your staff, "If you don't come to work on Saturday, don't bother showing up for work on Sunday."*

**Waste the entire first day back after New Year's by sitting around reading all 365 pages of everyone's new page-a-day calendars.**

If you are considering becoming an entrepreneur, first go out and get an entrepreneur's aptitude test from Inc. or Success magazine. If you get a perfect score, then go ahead—become an entrepreneur. If not, forget it.

*Dodge new assignments by walking briskly around the office with a stack of papers and a worried look.*

**Remember the maxim: "He who acts as his own lawyer saves a boatload in legal fees."**

Make a "tickler file" by taping a feather to a manila folder. Tickle the backs of people's necks when they owe you something.

*Give departing colleagues a gift basket full of pilfered office supplies as a going-away present.*

Give your boss *The Complete Idiot's Guide to Managing People* or *Managing for Dummies*. Tell him the bookstore was out of *The Total Asshole's Guide to Management*.

*Bend, fold, spindle, and mutilate.*

*Go faster. Work harder.*
*Do more. Faster, faster, faster.*
*More, more, more. Hurry up!*

**Subscribe to lots of free trade magazines. Reading them is a good way to avoid work while appearing busy.**

When someone leaves to exercise at lunch, cast them a suspicious look that says, "You're going to go to the gym, change, work out, shower, dry your hair, get dressed, grab lunch, do your errands, and still put in a full day's work. *Riiiight.*"

*Tuck a spare protractor, letter opener, and bookmark in your suitcase. You never know when you might need them on the road.*

**Suggest that beer be put in the soda machine.**

*Think of the telephone as an irresistible tyrant that must be answered every time it rings, no matter what you are doing.*

**Surprise your boss by decluttering and organizing his desk while he is out.**

*At the twilight of your life—on your deathbed in fact—the sentiment you are most likely to have is: "Why didn't I attend more business meetings? Now it's too late. Curse you, cruel fate! So much time spent with family, so few business meetings!"*

*Don't learn how to forward calls within your office. Make people who mistakenly reach you redial.*

**Think of a customer's complaint as a gift. A rotten, stinky gift that you wish he had kept to himself.**

**Wear a lead apron around the office to protect yourself from computer radiation.**

*While your boss gives you instructions, stare vacantly at a paper clip as you twist it into a free-form sculpture. When he finishes, say, "You talking at me?"*

Lots of people write memos to the file. Try writing memos to people *from* the file.

To:  Scott
From:  The File

Your recent memo to me was a joke. Never before have I received such a thinly disguised cover-your-ass memo.

Begin presentations with a joke. Self-deprecating humor is best. In fact, try to completely degrade yourself. Regale them for twenty minutes with jokes about your weight problem, hair loss, marital woes, and sexual inadequacies.

*Lock the rest rooms.*
*Make visitors beg for the key.*

When riding the elevator
with a person in a big hurry,
say, "Ya gotta slow down.
Stop and smell the roses."
Then push all the buttons
and wink before getting off.

Greet the security guard with "Mornin', Captain Waterpistol. Catch any evildoers today?"

*Hold an after-work seminar for colleagues on "Healing Your Inner Shame."*

*Holiday shopping needn't be a chore. Just grab your family some trinkets at the airport gift shop and order some of that fine merchandise from the in-flight magazine.*

**End all face-to-face interaction. Only communicate by e-mail.**

**If you cross your fingers
while signing a contract,
it is not enforceable.**

*If your boss asks you to make
a PERT chart, tell him, "I'll
make a chart all right, but I
can't guarantee it will be pert,
racy, or even a tad saucy."*

**Treat all consultants
as inherently evil.**

*Strategic vacation planning:
If your boss takes vacation
the first two weeks of July,
schedule yours for the last two
weeks. You've just dodged
him for a month!*

*Produce a CD-ROM of your "greatest memos of all time" and try to peddle it at flea markets.*

**March into the CEO's office, proclaim that you are indispensable, and demand a raise. CEOs respect chutzpah.**

*Generally lie to your boss.*
*Always lie to your boss's boss.*

**Wear stiff shoes to work.
Comfortable feet are the
devil's playground.**

It's better to succeed at some plodding, mundane task than to fail at something bold and new.

*Schedule a "critical all-hands meeting" for December 24 at 5:00 P.M. Then don't bother to show up.*

Ask coworkers mysterious
questions, scribble
on a clipboard, and
vaguely mutter about
"psychological profiles."

*Start each day by
assigning your boss a long
list of action items.*

*Introduce yourself to business acquaintances you've met many times before as though you are meeting them for the first time.*

**In meetings, absentmindedly tear, twist, and shred the agenda like it's the label from a beer bottle.**

*Play hard to get with headhunters.*

**Print all your e-mails and have your secretary type a memo summarizing them for you.**

Reduce travel expenses by having your staff ride Greyhound, share hotel rooms, brown-bag their meals, and drive "Rent-A-Wreck" cars. You, however, should take limos, fly the Concorde, and stay in the presidential suite.

**The more approval
signatures on a document,
the more carefully each
person reads it before signing.**

*Turn the office kitchen faucet
on full blast and stare at it,
muttering, "Useless, useless."*

*Ignore your intuition;
trust expert advice.*

**Volunteer to change the
copier toner cartridge.
Sit on the floor and split
it open with a hammer,
spilling toner everywhere.
Then walk away saying,
"I didn't do it."**

**Tell your staff to face their desks inward so you can see what's on their computers as you walk by.**

*Give your boss a thick report with hundreds of pages of "All work and no play makes Jack a dull boy."*

When your boss talks to
you, drum your fingers, tap
your foot, glance at your
watch, and yawn. Signal
that the conversation is over
by clamping your hands
over your ears and saying,
"La-la-la-la. La-la-la-la."

When a business acquaintance asks if you would like some coffee, say, "Why, yes! I'll have a grande, extra shot, skim, Swiss-water-process decaffeinated, hazelnut-flavored, coarsely ground, Italian roast latté with two packs of Sweet 'n Low, a dash of cinnamon, and a dollop of whipped cream, served at 140 degrees in a preheated mug and two chocolate-covered almond biscotti. And, of course, I'll need written documentation that the bean purveyor did not exploit the indigenous people who grew them."

When your boss asks if you're free for a meeting at such-and-such o'clock, say, "Sorry, that's no good for me. I've got a meeting at the watercooler to discuss last night's VH-1 special."

*Call computer support lines and ask where the "any" key is.*

*The only feedback employees need is criticism. Those slackers constantly pat themselves on the back.*

**Go to a backed-up fast-food restaurant's drive-thru at lunch hour and pay for your meal in pennies.**

*Before giving a presentation, take a moment to sense your queasy stomach, pounding heart, dry mouth, and trembling hands. Gaze at the judgmental, unfriendly faces in the audience. Reflect on your unpreparedness. Now off you go.*

**The moment you get in that rental car, you *are* Mario Andretti.**

*When you miss deadlines, say your Palm Pilot's batteries ran out, preventing you from accessing your "to-do" list.*

*Go to work with a phlegmy cough.*

**No matter what your workload, complain to your supervisor that you are swamped. Before you know it, it's Snickers bars and Solitaire from 9 to 5.**

Join every pyramid scheme that comes your way. One of them is bound to pay off.

*If you have to use the rest room during a business lunch, take your plate with you so "no one steals your vittles."*

Some good questions to ask during job interviews are:

- "Does your health plan cover sex change operations?"

- "Would it be a problem if I'm angry most of the time?"

- "When is Naked Day at this company?"

- "Will your relocation plan cover shipping my cinder block collection?"

- "Would it help my chances if I tattooed the company logo on my chest?"

*Bang on a calculator and nod your head while making personal phone calls to make them look work-related.*

**When interviewers ask about your weaknesses, explore the topic in great depth.**

Speak like a gangsta rapper at work: "Yo Mac Daddy, we doin' dis meetin' G-style. I here representin' da department of dead presidents. 'Sup wit yo marketin' posse, homey?"

*Fold your memos into origami animals before delivering them.*

Empower employees to make their own decisions, but start 'em real slow. Let them decide which side of the desk to store their pens and how many sugars for their coffee. In six months they may be ready to decide whether to turn off the computer or the monitor first.

Guzzle a cooler full of non-alcoholic beers at the next staff meeting. There's no company policy against *that*.

*Remember: A person is a success if he gets up in the morning, goes to bed at night, and in between makes a lot of money.*

*Never wear a gray, navy,
or pinstriped suit to a job
interview. And never, ever
wear a white or blue shirt.
Try a short-sleeve shirt
with a tie for a relaxed yet
powerful combination.*

**Duck out of dull meetings
by manually chirping
your pager.**

**Slavishly follow the management fad of the month.**

*Put lots of toys and puzzles on your desk. They'll distract your boss when he comes to give you assignments and make him forget why he came.*

**Never let customers
know how long they will
have to wait to be served.**

*Turn the slide projector's
fan off, but leave its light
on. Mmm, crispy.*

Resumes are a lot like puppies: the cuter, the better. Load yours up with gimmicks, double entendres, clip art, and personal information. Print it on scented lavender paper, typeset in calligraphy.

Manage the bonus cycle. If your performance review is in June, then surge in May and June, and slack off from July through April. Managers only remember what you've done for them *lately*.

*Praise your staff by patting them on the head and saying, "Good boy" or "Good girl."*

*Stealing office supplies to boot-strap your home-based business can be a real boost, especially if your home-based business is selling stolen office supplies.*

**Play out your unresolved childhood pain at work. Be a victim, an ogre, a martyr!**

*Get bogged down in corporate politics and administrative minutiae. Let the products take care of themselves.*

**Ask someone doing a small copying job if you can break in with your big job.**

Lucite cubes commemorating business deals are the Holy Grail. You can work people to death if they think there's a Lucite cube in it for them.

*Contract paralysis by analysis.*

**Drive like a banshee in the company car, especially if it has a "How Am I Driving?" sticker on it.**

*Wear the same clothes to work all week.*

*Paste your advertising flyers to car windows in supermarket parking lots. It's not worth your time if people can just yank 'em off without reading them.*

**Use action verbs in your resume, like "demoralized," "bungled," and "wrecked."**

*Use your desktop as an archive for long-term document storage, while your desk drawers function primarily as a repository for condiment packages.*

**If your boss tries to sit with you at lunch, tell him, "Sorry, you can't sit here. This is the *cool* table."**

Drain a competitor's fax
machine by faxing him
an endless loop made
from two sheets of paper
taped together.

*Come home late after hitting
happy hour with coworkers and
tell your wife you were busy
drinking "work-related beers."*

## Let Ms. Rosie Scenario do your forecasting.

*Want to slack off but not get fired? Always keep a jar of candy on your desk. No one fires the candy man.*

*Page people, then walk
away from your phone.*

**When asked what salary
you are looking for, it's best
to start really low so you
don't frighten them off.
Then talk your way up
from there.**

Savvy travelers know these tips:

- **Direct dial long-distance calls from your hotel room.**

- **Accept rental-car insurance.**

- **Leave your laptop unattended in airport lounges.**

Switch from a filing system to a *piling* system. Construct teetering skyscrapers of paper.

*Request vast quantities of special-order office supplies in a vain attempt to get organized. Then immediately discard them like yesterday's coffee.*

*Stare inquisitively at colleagues'
facial imperfections. Demand
a complete explanation for
all zits, hickeys, scratches,
and cold sores.*

**Tempt the computer gods:
Work for a long time
without saving your file
during a thunderstorm.
Without a surge suppressor.**

When asked by an interviewer what your salary requirements are, chuckle and say, "Well, at least as much as you make."

*Spend hours every day organizing the office sports betting pool.*

At the end of a negotiation, tell your counterpart how much you were *willing* to pay. Let him know how much money he left on the table.

*Frame a photo of your boss and display it prominently on your desk.*

Replenish your supplies by raiding your neighbor's office. It's easier than walking all the way to the supply room. On the other hand, your stuff should be labeled "Borrow Me and Die, Jagoff!"

*Mount a paper shredder on
your trash can and put it on
your desk. Label it "In Box."
Pile a bunch of crossword
puzzles in your "Out Box."*

Set your answering machine
to pick up after twenty
rings. Only the persistent
deserve to be rewarded.

Display an unnatural fear of staple removers. Say that you were once tortured mercilessly with one by a Colombian drug lord and the experience still haunts you.

*Say good-bye to everyone in the building each night before you leave.*

When your boss screws
up, try to fire him.
Or at least dock his pay.

*Decorate your office with
posters like "I Hate Mondays,"
"I'm Too Cute to Work," and
"Wake Me When It's Friday."*

*Always accept invitations to volunteer your time and assume new social obligations.*

**Tell your staff to forgo their dreams and aspirations and walk around saying, "I love my job. I love my job."**

*Telemarket your product
to people at 3:00 A.M.*

**Moving day coming up?
Don't lug those boxes by
yourself. Strongly "suggest"
that your staff help out.**

Give your staff multiple
jobs at once but don't let
them know the priority.
Make a game out of it;
let them guess.

*No matter what your boss tells
you, just say, "That's fine."*

Volunteer to do all the arrangements for the company Christmas party. Then hold it at McDonald's Playland and charge $50 a ticket.

*If you have special instructions for a job, wait until the job is almost finished before divulging them.*

*Whenever you are right
and your boss is wrong,
do a "victory dance" and
shout, "In your face!"*

**Return your rental car
bone-dry, but tell the
clerk you filled it up.**

*Every time you send a fax,
call to see if it arrived.*

Give your coworkers
nicknames and refer to
them only by these names.
"Finish that report yet,
Derwood?" "Nice
presentation, Slicky-Boy."

# Schedule meetings
# for 2:17 P.M.

*Bring your secretary a present
when you return from a trip,
like . . . a huge pile of
receipts to sort out.*

*On every purchase request*
*mark the "need date"*
*as "last week."*

**After a job interview,
it is customary to call the
personnel office every
hour to see if they have
made a decision yet.**

**Winning isn't everything. *Whining* is everything.**

*There is a limited pool of success out there. Every time a friend or colleague triumphs, it detracts from the glory remaining for you.*

*Chase work tail. Dip your pen in the company ink. Get your pink where you get your green. Download your laptop into the company software. Take advantage of your coworker's perks. Swim in the secretarial pool. Plug and play in your neighborhood network. Fish off the company pier. Get your meat where you get your bread.*

*Propose daily drug tests
for all employees.*

**Have underlings fetch you
rocks for your amusement.
When they return, say,
"I don't like this rock.
Fetch me another."**

When engineers start spewing mumbo-jumbo, rein them in with, "Slow down, Poindexter! I'm as confused as a hungry baby in a topless bar."

**Conduct a nightly company-wide pen inventory.**

Try these catchy slogans for your business:

- "You can buy better, but you can't pay more!"

- "We're slow, but we do poor work!"

- "Sure, you could pay less, but then we wouldn't make as much money!"

Harangue coworkers with the details of your latest diet. It is your duty to inform them about every piece of food you eat and every calorie you burn.

*Believe the dealer's invoice.*

*Qualify all your remarks.
"I may be totally off base
on this, but I sort of feel
that maybe we ought to
think about . . . "*

**Tape the hang-up button
of your boss's phone
down, then call him.**

*In a properly functioning office, executives should futz around, typing their own memos, while secretaries spend all day in meetings.*

**Meddle in other people's responsibilities while completely ignoring your own.**

*Next time you're driving,
see if you can drink scalding
coffee, change radio stations,
eat a jelly doughnut, talk on
the phone, switch lanes, steer
with your knee, shush the kids,
and flip off the guy behind
you all at the same time.*

**Delete the system files on your computer to make more room for your MP3s.**

*Mispronounce people's names. Make a game of it. Try to fashion something a fifth grader would find hysterical.*

*When conducting a job interview, check the applicant's pulse and say, "Okay, you're qualified."*

**Delegate all your work to your secretary, leaving you more time to travel, play corporate politics, and lobby for raises and promotions.**

*Sow despair, frustration, and anxiety through the office.*

If someone disagrees with you in a meeting, discredit them with, "That sounds suspiciously like something Adolf Hitler might have said."

Keep your answers to interview questions short. One word, "yes/no" responses are best.

*Remember: The more you push the elevator button, the faster it comes.*

Answer your phone with a long, rambling spiel like, "Good morning and thank you very much for dialing the award-winning Nimrod Hotel where serving the customer is always our number-one priority. At Nimrod we put you first because we know your time is precious. My name is Michelle and I'll be your customer service representative. How may I help you this morning, Sir or Madam?"

# Think "inside the box."

*At business conferences, go around the room grabbing two strangers, saying, "Random guy, I'd like you to meet some other guy," and then dashing off.*

*Greet casual business acquaintances of the same sex with "hello kisses."*

**When your boss enters your office, leap to your feet and salute him.**

**Burst into closed-door meetings and hysterically shout: "Soylent Green is made of *PEOPLE*!"**

*Hog the copier and let no one "play through."*

*Treat women in the workplace like fragile china.*

**When you quit a job for another one, tell your old coworkers they are fools for staying at such a terrible place.**

Handy tips for the international business traveler:

- In Japan, show the inside of your mouth during conversations.

- In India, gifts of leather are appreciated.

- In China, give clocks as gifts.

- In Saudi Arabia, sit with the soles of your feet showing.

- In Muslim countries, shake with your left hand.

*A proper business handshake should be as gentle as you would hold a dried leaf.*

**Every time your boss starts talking to you, throw a Tic-Tac in his mouth.**

*Carry a folder labeled "My Grudge List" containing perceived injustices and slights committed against you by your colleagues. Carry it with you and review it often and conspicuously. Scribble in it furiously during performance reviews.*

**Presume that plump customers are pregnant and ask when they are due.**

*Ask your secretary to give you wake-up calls after lunch.*

*Be listed first in the yellow pages. Change your company name from "Smith Hardware" to "Aaaaaasmith Hardware." Claim it's Hawaiian and demand that people pronounce each "a."*

**Become a slave to technology.**

**Hire outsiders for plum positions. Never promote from within.**

*Don't sweat the small stuff. Unfortunately, your problems are all the big stuff. Happy sweating.*

*While the boss talks to a coworker in a meeting, visibly yawn at the coworker to get him to yawn at the boss.*

**Put a piece of rotten fruit in the office kitchen and label it "Do NOT Remove." See how many months it stays there.**

When the elevator stops, crumple to the ground as if the jolt took you by surprise. Shout to your fellow passengers, "Didn't you feel that? The gravity suddenly got *very* strong in here!"

Put $10 in a Swiss bank account just so you can brag about having one.

**Call your clients collect. Send them letters postage due.**

*Staple your documents ten times. In the center of the page.*

*Wink at female executives and say, "Fetch some coffee, will ya, Sweetie?"*

When your staff complains about their paltry bonuses, say that you thought they wanted a big "bone us!" Then lecture them on the importance of clear communications.

Send an e-mail to everyone saying there's free pizza in the kitchen. When they show up, sit there next to an empty pizza box, licking your chops, and say, "You'll have to be a whole lot quicker than that."

When choosing your first
job out of college, pick
whichever one offers
the best accidental
dismemberment plan.

*Tell your boss you need a
high-end $15,000 Silicon
Graphics workstation to
type your memos.*

When your boss asks what you've done today, say, "Well, the pushpin brigade led by General Glue Stick has crushed the paper clip uprising, but Colonel Wite-Out still won't surrender Fort Keyboard."

*Never tell your secretary where you are going or when you'll be back.*

**It is better to own four $200 suits than one $800 suit.**

*Fast forward: your retirement day. Riding down the elevator with a colleague for the last time. He asks what the highlight of your career was. You stare at him for a moment, misty-eyed, then walk out muttering, "What a waste, what a waste!"*

# ABOUT THE AUTHOR

Steve Altes works as an actor, model, writer, and speaker. His participatory adventure essays have appeared in magazines like *Salon, P.O.V., Tear Sheet, Capital Style* and the *Washington Post*. He is the author of *The Little Book of Bad Business Advice* and has appeared in over three-hundred print ads and TV commercials. He and his wife live in Virginia. He can be reached at stevealtes@aol.com.